HOUSE CROSSING

Other Works by the Author

Monographs

Myth as Argument: The Bṛhaddevatā as Canonical Commentary in *Religionges-chichtliche Versuche und Vorarbeiten*. Lawrence Sullivan, Fritz Graf and Hans G. Kippenberg, Series editors. Berlin: DeGruyter Mouton, in collaboration with Harvard University, Center for the Study of World Religions, 1996.

Bringing the Gods to Mind: Mantra and Ritual in Early Indian Sacrifice. Berkeley: University of California Press, 2006.

Who Owns Religion? Scholars and their Publics in the Late 20th Century. Chicago: University of Chicago Press, in press, forthcoming 2019.

Edited Volumes

Editor, with Brian Black, *The Dialogical in Ancient Indian Religions: Hindu, Buddhist, and Jain Traditions.* London: Ashgate Press, 2015.

Editor, with David Haberman, *Notes from a Mandala: Essays in the Indian History of Religions in Honor of Wendy Doniger.* University of Delaware Press, 2010.

Editor, with Edwin Bryant. *The Indo-Aryan Controversy: Evidence, History, and Politics.* London: Routledge/Taylor Francis Press, 2005.

Editor. *Jewels of Authority: Women and Textual Tradition in Hindu India.* New York: Oxford University Press, 2002.

Editor, with Wendy Doniger. *Myth and Method.* Series in Religion and Culture. Charlottesville: University Press of Virginia, 1996.

Editor. *Authority, Anxiety and Canon: Essays in Vedic Interpretation.* Albany: State University of New York Press, 1994.

Translations

The Bhagavad Gita Harmondsworth, England: Penguin Press, 2008.

Poetry

Angel's Task: Poems in Biblical Time. Barrytown: Station Hill Press, 2011.

Fire's Goal: Poems from a Hindu Year. Seattle: White Clouds Press, 2003.

HOUSE CROSSING

LAURIE L. PATTON

Station Hill

BARRYTOWN

Published by Station Hill of Barrytown, the publishing project of the Institute for Publishing Arts, Inc., 120 Station Hill Road, Barrytown, NY 12507, New York, a not-for-profit, tax-exempt organization [501(c)(3)].

 This publication is supported in part by grants from the New York State Council on the Arts, a state agency.

Online catalogue: www.stationhill.org
e-mail: publishers@stationhill.org

Cover and interior design by Susan Quasha
Cover photo by Laurie L. Patton

Library of Congress Cataloging-in-Publication Data

Names: Patton, Laurie L., 1961- author.
Title: House crossing / Laurie L. Patton.
Description: Barrytown, NY : Station Hill Press, [2018]
Identifiers: LCCN 2017048477 | ISBN 9781581771671 (pbk.)
Subjects: LCSH: Houses—Poety. | Space (Architecture)—Poetry.
Classification: LCC PS3616.A9265 A6 2018 | DDC 811/.6—dc23
LC record available at https://lccn.loc.gov/2017048477

Manufactured in the United States of America

In Memory of
Gaston Bachelard

Acknowledgments

So many have inspired and taught. Here is an inadequate naming of first readers: Shalom Goldman, Gwyneth Lewis, Velcheru Narayana Rao, Richard Chess, Rosemary Magee, Angelika Bammer, Leslie Taylor, Elizabeth Gallu, Ruby Lal, Lynne Huffer, Leslie Harris, David Shulman, Shlomit Finkelstein, David Finkelstein, Rachel McDermott, Roy Tzohar, Leela Prasad, Lila Porterfield, Cat Kemmett, Caitlyn Patton, and Chakravarthi Ram-Prasad.

Versions of the poems in this book have appeared in the following literary journals:

"Closet" in *Westview* 32.1 (Winter, 2016)

"Mother House" in *Licking River Review* (Fall, 2015)

"Beams" in *The Alembic* (Spring 2015)

"Fountain" and "House" in *Women Arts Quarterly* 5.2 (2015)

"Chimney" in *Tulane Review* (Fall, 2013*)*

"Attic" in *Forge* 7.3 *(*Winter, 2014)

"Eaves" in *Stickman Review* 12.2 (Fall, 2013)

"Floor" in *DeComp Magazine* (November, 2013)

"Mantel" in *Sanskrit* Vol. 44 *(2013)*

"Stair" in *Reed Magazine Vol. 66* (2013)

"Corner" in *Bluestem* (September 2013)

"Window II" *in Green Hills Literary Lantern* XXIV (2013)

"Window," "Cellar," "Bricks" "Porch" "Hallway," in *Grey Sparrow Journal* 11 (Winter, 2012)

Contents

INTRODUCTION

Gaston Bachelard entitled his phenomenological work, *The Poetics of Space*, and his work does indeed "take lessons from poets."[1] Bachelard's philosophy moves between the minute analysis of a single poem and the larger literary theory that encompasses an entire genre of literature.[2] Since its publication in 1958, *The Poetics of Space* has become what Raine Daston calls an "undead text"—one of those texts whose popularity endures long after it should have gone out of intellectual fashion.

House Crossing arises out of a straightforward observation about the endurance of Bachelard's work: if a philosophy is good enough, and I believe Bachelard's is, then it does not only comment on poetry, but can give rise to poetry as well. The simple poetry of houses seemed to me to be the most authentic response to *The Poetics of Space*. Our 21st century lives are such that we have become less and less shaped by our dwelling places. In that light, Bachelard's words seem particularly salient: "The virtues of shelter are so simple, so deeply rooted in our unconscious that they may be recaptured through mere mention."[3]

The poems in *House Crossing* are based on many houses, none of them described completely as they exist or existed in history,

---

[1] Bachelard, Gaston, *The Poetics of Space*, (Boston: Beacon Press, 1994) p. 56; First printed as *La Poétique de L'Espace* (Paris: Press Universitaires de France, 1958).

[2] McHale, Brian (1994) "Whatever Happened to Descriptive Poetics?" in *The Point of Theory: Practices of Cultural Analysis* (Eds., Mieke Bal & Inge E. Boer). Amsterdam: Amsterdam University Press, p. 59

[3] Ibid.

but all of them evocative of personal histories—my own and others'. They emerge from what Bachelard calls "the real houses of memory."[4] They are contemplative readings of simple architectural elements—hall, cupola, corner. I have stayed away from furniture or objects and let the geometry of intimacy speak for itself. The body responds to the shape of home, and that response becomes a poem. And the poem, I hope, becomes a transformation, a "crossing" to another way of seeing, as simple and complicated as crossing to the other side of a room.

---

[4] Bachelard, *Poetics*, p. 12
[5] Ibid., p. 13

CELLAR

Today the tile man came
to fix the stair.
He told us
about the river
that runs below the house.

Twenty feet under,
a green current
pushes through.

I've heard it.
The air has always moved
a little faster
near the porch.
In the winter,
the pillars settle.
In the summer,
the mosquitoes swarm
for no reason.

I've smelt it.
I've lit lamps
to cover
the stink of swamp,
and made excuses
to the guests
as they stepped over
the threshold.

Ten years ago,
I would have called
the tile man's friends
to help.
I would have watched,
eagerly,
as they climbed
into my cellar
to measure, sniff, and mutter
about the value of cement.

Their boots
would have reminded me
to make love
later in the day.

But now
I won't call those men.

Let the mosquitoes nest.
Let the green push
of the river
enter my dreams.

And when I lie down,
and the heat rises
in these unruly limbs,
let the current be
a beckoning bed
soothing these veins
in cool, brown
tributaries of rest.

PORCH

—for Angelika

On my porch,
people say what they want.

I don't remember the first part
of the poet's sentence,
but I remember the second:

*"…and I will tell you when I find
some kind of order…"*

Right then, a firefly
behind her head
singed the night.

She could call it
luciferase
or
longing.

Either way,
in that insect's light
order became
a trembling lure
among the jagged stars.

BRICKS

The earth was perfect,
until one day
they had to make an altar.
"Make bricks!"
the old gods said.
And so they did.
"Make an altar
in the shape of a bird!"
Their sweat
poured down
on the earth
while they arranged
the dusty wings.
"Not good enough,"
said the gods.
So they started again.

My father was perfect
until one day
he asked me
to help him
lay the bricks
for a path.
"We didn't go down
six inches,"
he said,
"and your grandfather
is coming soon."

We got the last brick in
before the old engineer
got out of the car.
He handed me
a cinnamon candy
and looked down
at the ground.
He smoothed some sand
between the bricks
with his shoe.
Without looking up,
he said,
"Did you go down
six inches?"
My father nodded.

My garden was perfect
until one day
the bricks got moved.
The roots
of the peony bush
red and rotting
had pushed them
into the air.
The hose slithered
between them,
hissing water.

I kicked them
back into place,
secretly hoping
they would move again
in the night.

WINDOW I

The old window
in the farmhouse
is always
part of our story
when we tell each other
about the ghosts.

Perhaps it is
an accident
of our imaginations,
like the greenish glass itself—
pontil marks
air bubbles
slight irregularities.

But the one looking
through the glass
two hundred years ago,
squinting to see
the fields beyond,
pressed her head against
its imperfections
and wished them gone.

She longed to see
her daughter near the horse—
Was it moving
as she mounted?
her son with a basket of wheat—
How many sheaves?

But her questions
were caught
in the waves of bottled green,
only now to be released
in the hazy shapes
of our whispered tales.

WINDOW II

He landed
in the storm
and spread
his moth wings
on the dark window.

His underbelly
was the size of
of my finger.
He pulsed green,
then blue,
then orange.

I put my hand
on the glass.
His wings trembled.
I tapped on the pane.

"This is not
a source of light"
I whispered.
"This is just
a dark window."

He was still there.
in the morning.
His wings
had withstood
the night,
his colors
finely dusted
by the winds.

"All right," I said to him.
"This is not
just a dark window.
It is a source of light
I cannot see."

HALLWAY

My mother and I
have been having
a conversation.

Noah's ark stands
at the end of our hallway—
doll-sized, in painted pine.
The Noah-doll leans on the gunwale,
his arms outstretched.

My mother had arranged
all the animals
in straight rows of pairs.
That way,
at the end of the hall
past the rugs
and the old stoves
and encyclopedias
with fraying corners,
my mother sees order.

"They like being in rows,"
she says.
"And Noah is orchestrating
all of them inside."

One night I snuck down
and made chaos instead:
I piled zebras on turtles
and twisted geese over tigers
and separated rabbits
from their mates.
I made them run in all directions.

"Noah is desperately trying
to get their attention,"
I told my mother.

That way,
at the end of the hall,
past the old planks
and brass lamps,
and straight curtains,
I see effort and sweat
and the longing to bring
panicked creatures
in from the storm.

What we see
at the end of the hall
is the difference between
rest and restlessness,
nightmare and dream.

I learned later
that there were no windows
in the ark,
but only a pearl
that glowed by day
so that everyone could see.

FLOOR

After he smears
his face with ash,
and presses his cheek
to the floor,
what does Job see?

Perhaps tiny worlds
are the only ones
that grief can see,
when the human-sized
weight of loss
pushes us groundward.

Perhaps he is given
the eyes of a child:
the whorls
in the wooden planks
become traces of wind,
and the lines
between the tiles
are teeming roads,
trafficked by mites.

STAIR

Photographs
of our mothers
follow
the staircase—
six generations.
of them.

Some wear
bridal lace.
Others twinkle.
Others look grim.
(Smiling
has only been
customary
in the last two
generations.)

In our nightly ascent
toward dreams,
we count
seven pine planks.
Each step
cradles our feet.
A mother
is with us
each time
we bend our knees.

As we climb,
we choose
a single act
from the multitude
that propelled
their days:

This mother
never spoke
of her divorce
from the husband
who went to jail
for disorderly conduct

This mother
drew beautifully
and went away
for a long time
so no one knew
where she was

This mother
tried to play
the piano
but took refuge
in Adam's Nervine
to recover her wits

This mother
sometimes peeked
under the bed
to look at the whip
her father kept
just in case

This mother
was afraid to go
out of the house
where wide open spaces
could kill

This mother
ate so little
she thought
she had mastered
the universe

A landing
before we make
the final climb
toward sleep
and sky.

There, we sit
and ponder
the maternal
possibilities.

ARCHWAY

Edward Abbey looked up
from the sand
and wanted
an answer
from Delicate Arch.

Under the archway
to the kitchen,
we watched
the steam
from the pots
travel through
and condense
in its curve.

We tried
to hang plants
from its sides,
but the brackets
did not hold.

We passed
underneath,
and pressed
our small palms

against its plaster,
waiting for a sound.

Our arch
did not require
explanation.

If we dwelt
underneath it
long enough,
it might become
a curved body
encircling us.

CORNER

Two hundred years ago
two walls and a floor
were smoothed
by the disciplined love
of the lathe.

The hands that held it
did not know
they were joining
the axes
of heaven and earth.

One hundred years ago
a soldier returned
from his prison,
but could not bear
the open space
of a room.
He turned
to the corner
for solace,
and sat for hours,
cradled in its lines.

Fifty years ago
I stayed there too.
First, I stretched out
my arms to you,
holding them forever
in the perfect shape
of a triangle.

When you walked away
I stopped
my exercise
in human geometry,
and settled
into these walls.
Their golden wood
embraced body
and cheek
and tired bone.

"Keep walking,"
I said to you
from the corner
as you became
smaller and smaller
in the distance.

The joining
of heaven and earth
would have to wait
for another day.

CLOSET

The upper closet
had a tiny window—
latticed, and round.
Its patch of light
(sometimes gray,
sometimes yellow),
lifted us skyward.

We went there often
to be wrapped
by the hemlines
of winter coats
still smelling of pine,
to be held
by the rows of shoes,
their leathery colors
barely visible
in the light.
Once we were cradled
in fleece and wool,
we craned our necks
to see the moon.

One evening,
as we were whispering
among the coats,
our father the surgeon
put a candle
on the windowsill.

We asked him
what it was for.

He said
it was there
to call the dog,
now dead for
seven months,
all the way home.

MANTEL

At twilight,
the two ends
of the mantelpiece
became big shoulders,
inviting
all the old spirits
to lean in and sigh.

After sunset,
my grandfather
often felt
someone tapping
on his back
when he rested
against it.

Today,
you give me
a painted tile
where two figures
carry a branch
on their shoulders
to hold up
the basket
between them.

The pole is bent
with the weight.
The figures
look tired
and gentle.

As you watch me
unwrap it,
you tell me
it reminds you
of our marriage.

I keep asking—
first my grandfather,
and now you:

Can pieces of wood—
carved ledges,
smooth branches,
really hold up
the longings
of the world?

CHIMNEY

When they were thirty,
he bought her the house
with the striped chimney—
an eighteenth century sign
that a Tory lived within.

Not thinking of revolution,
but escape from despair
she was charmed by the stripe
and healed by the trees.

"Don't strain yourself,"
she says later
to his eighty-year-old frame,
only half visible
as he slides
into the fireplace
to open the flu,
shut since the last time
he gave her a party.

He pulls it downward.
Two birds' nests
and a petrified squirrel
fall on his face
and shoulders.
She screams
and then laughs.
The fire is lit.
The party continues.

At the Taj Mahal
he says to her,
"I bought you the house,
but a marble tomb
would be too much,
even for me."

"Don't strain yourself,"
she says.
"An old chimney
is all the monument
I need."

ATTIC

The attic
was not a place
where shafts of light
danced on the beams
and people ran fast
up the stairs
to play.

Its dark doors
only opened
when my brother
needed a suitcase
to leave for Arizona
(and for good);
when my father
longed for pinwheels
on the fourth of July;
when my cousin
wanted to use
an old baptismal gown
to bury her child.

They opened again
yesterday evening.
My mother
dragged out
all the boxes
before the final sale
of the house.

Her hands shook.
The air smelled
of rotting pine.

The last box
held very little
except a drawing
with my initials
on the bottom.

"When did you do this?"
my mother asked.

"Sixth grade,"
I answered.
"Mrs. Dougherty
asked us
to draw ourselves
when we were fifty."

It was 1973.
I drew an old lady.
Her hair was greenish white,
the color of grass
at the first break of dawn,
and each cheek
was a different color.
She wore
a psychedelic shawl
pinned with a brooch.

"She looks like me,"
my mother said.

The gravel crunched
as the movers
pulled up
into the driveway.

"We'd better
keep her, then,"
I said.

"Yes," said my mother.
"Before she is sold."

EAVES

We must have thought
that bats lived lives
as miniatures
of our own.
In the blue
of the morning,
we used to peer up
into their cradles
to see if they slept.
Restless at twilight,
they left the shelter
of loving corners
for the arcs
of open space,
and returned
to fold their hunger,
not yet sated,
into the wings
of the night.

BEAMS

In our kitchen
they were vaults
of darkened sky—
their splinters stars
to be gathered
by our hands.

You lifted me up
so I could touch them.

Perhaps it was then
I began to believe
sky was possible
because of the circle
of your arms.

FOUNTAIN

On the day I die
and my heart
finally escapes
its beautiful cage
its pulses
scattered to the winds

let the young woman
watching the fountain
that morning
see a sudden surge
of splash and color
and greet it
with jubilation
as if it were lava
or witches' brew

let the little man
who opens
the draw bridge
at high noon
turn the crank
one more time
his body a happy flag
on the lever
as the gulls
sing the boats through

let last year's ghost,
waiting by the bed
finally quicken
her lover's dreams
so that he turns
and curls his hand
around nothing
in particular

let my heart roam free
for it has been pounding
against these bars
for so long

CEILING

One night
we finally asked
about the brown stain
above us
that caught our eye
every night
at dinner.

"Apple butter,"
our father said.
"We couldn't afford
real butter
during the war."

"My brother and I
were wrestling,
and I slammed it
down on the table,
and it shot into the air."

Later that night,
we raced out
with flashlights
to shine the beams
toward the stars,
and watched them
as they landed
in the closer comfort
of the clouds.

HOUSE FROM A DISTANCE

On a train
in a country
where I knew some,
but not all,
of the words,
I saw yellow flowers
spiraling off
the embankment.

As they sped by,
I wanted to say,
forsythia,
but they could have been
gorse, or *daylily*,
or *snapdragon.*
I would have struggled
for those words, too.

Then it appeared
in the green swathes
of the window—
someone's house,
perfect as a pocket.

I knew
behind its sweet walls
there were aunts waiting,
cousins
who bounced balls
in greeting,
baths
with wet footprints
on the tiles,
vines
whose tendrils curled
like small hands
around fences.

The infinite second
exploded then.
The train flew on.
I watched
the flowers mutely,
no longer struggling
to utter their name.

SHELF

The bottles lay
in bright piles
on the second shelf:
dog's eye drops
brother's aspirin
cat's penicillin
mother's powder.

I dreamt one night
that Asclepius' hand
had thrown them together,
in a frenzy to make
a garden of remedies
we could pluck at will.

But it was your hand,
not Asclepius—
your longing
to gather all illnesses
unto yourself.

Then all creatures
under your roof
could come searching
for solace
in your rooms.

WINDOWSILL

We talked for hours
about the scene
in that film
where the poet sat
on the windowsill
choosing between
the dinner to honor
his literary life
and a sudden painful peace
on the hot street
ten floors below.

No one wanted
to see him
hurl himself streetward,
but he did.
We wondered
if he found
oblivion better.

Our choices
at the windowsill
are smaller ones:

Do we let
the dog's nose
rest there
in the evening,
though bats
could stream in
and get tangled
in our hair?

Do we raise
the old sash
used for years
by gnarled hands
so the sun can spread
into our blinded morning,
or do we sleep further
in the darkness?

Do we brave the night air
and all its cold questions
to let the cat in
as she clings
screaming silently
on the screen,
or do we make her return
to her prowling
amongst the owls?

In each case
there is no one
to tell us
which act
would hurl us
toward oblivion,
and which
would throw us back
into a warmer,
more difficult life.

DOORSTEP

Before you ask me
to come inside,
let me show you
this twilight color
that paints our skin in silver,
and makes us want
to drink the sky,
and gather the lights
in the darkened trees,
and run wild
through the furrows
of the wine-soaked earth,
until we fall
over your doorstep
into the smoothness
of sleep.

MOTHER HOUSE

Even though
she is now alive
I wonder
what kind of ghost
she will be.

I leave her house
to admire its shape
from the yard—
a beloved trapezoid,
and beyond it,
a sweet rectangular sea,
triangles of nests,
ovals of rock.

But the photos
of that day
are gray on gray.
The ghost
is already there,
I think,
and rush
to find something
to paint in
the colors.

WALL

We did not want
her last days
to be the Gulf War
on the Channel 9 news.

She began
to confuse the TV
with the hills
outside her window.
The yellowing shrubs
turned into taxis
in the desert.
The cool wind
that should have soothed her
became a hurricane
of sand.

She tried
to change the channel
by banging on the sill.
Yet the war kept coming.

Her time of peace
was the wall in between.
Staring blankly at it
was her privilege.
We thanked the wall
for mutely guiding her
to a quieter end.

Those desert fighters
never knew
they were actors
in another war.

Her granddaughters
soothed her limbs
with warm towels,
and absently swayed
to the cries
of the last geese
flying south
from the pond.

PILLAR

The house
was joyously not
our fathers' house.
It had six pillars,
brave, stout, and petulant,
on the splintering porch.

We threw bright rugs
and built fountains nearby.
We hung swings
that creaked
while the pillars
stayed silent.
We sliced cucumbers
and gathered lettuce
for feasts.
White chalk
dusted our sweaters
when we leaned against them,
careless and beaming.

Lot's wife
wanted to know
the fate
of her father's house.

And so she turned.
Some say
she saw God
in that turning.

Among pillars,
we forget
that our fathers
are always behind us,
as we run
from the smoldering fires
of all the houses
built before.

ROOF

ocean's gift
of triangle days

toes trace
leafy gutters
grey shingles
scratch thighs
arms slip
in windy sprays
hands follow
pebbled streams
salt falls
on open lips

night brings
harbors' mainsails
clang clang
clanging someone
home

SHED

When she turned eighty
we looked together
for white Lady Slippers
near Thoreau's cabin.
"It's just a shed," she told me.
"The Lady Slippers are the thing."

When she lost her breath
from the climb,
she didn't speak of it.
The white slippers
nodded and swayed
at her quiet gasping.

I wondered
whether Henry David
inspired her silence—
all his writing
coming down,
a century later,
to the single thing
she could not say:

His God-free prayer
that a dignified life
has, as its primary end,
a dignified death,
where streams ask us
to follow
their branches and eddies,
like his Maine canoe,
helpless and serene.

I looked down
at the forest floor,
noting that
her stockings
matched the pine.

ROOM

Waking at fifty,
I remembered
what cities
floated on the horizons
when waking at ten.

Crossing to them
was sailing in darkness
across oceans,
not floorboards,
the watery space of night
infinitely wide
after dreaming.

A spire in a cloud
surely meant London;
and the radio tower
was Paris beckoning.

Stumbling through the room
to open the window
was cavernous travel,
silent and dangerous.

Now I wake without
the memory of dreams:
what cities can possibly
call me?

CUPOLA

Because every book of art, be it a poem or a cupola, is
understandably a self-portrait of its author....

JOSEPH BRODSKY

Farmers know
cupolas are built
to admit light and air,
even laughter
when the skies darken.

I think of them
as overturned bowls
to catch the heat
of the prayers
before they fly out,
and scorch the roof
with their longing.

One October sunset
I walked by a church
with an open one.
The leaves poured in,
in windy rivers
of restless gold.
The cupola
could not hold them.

I tried to contain the vision
with a fervid report,
a lively tale, told
to tolerant friends
before the darkening skies.

The farmers knew
to be silent,
and bowed their heads
as the leaves rushed through.

WELL

I came early.

And in this,
all the dreams make sense—
dreams where I float,
remembering a past life,
a sweet tendril
that I still hold
curled in my hands

A woman
appears often—
a woman and a girl
hallelujah
she too is always
floating in a womb

She came first
as an old woman
tumbling from a closet
in a gulley,
draped in sadhu's cloth
turned away from the moon

Then as a younger one
lying in the watery reeds
near a hill
with perfect lilies
and a wind so sweet
it lifted her hair

Then she rested
in an island pool
with limpets and red algae
pale as a shell
undisturbed
by the storm

Then she stared
from within a grave,
peaceful and still
so that scholars
might discover
her perfect square
of a tomb

Like Miriam,
these women at the well
declare survival
the highest love of all

They are the holders
of the soul
that came early—
washed, fetal, ancient
hallelujah

DEMOLITION

I sold it
(a simple *yes*)
to a man on the phone.
I didn't stand
on the doorstep
with a rifle
as I thought I might.

I sold it
because I began
to think
of the next one.

I took the dogs
back to those woods
just after
the back hoes
had finished their work.

There lay
a globe of colors,
a moonrise of rubble.
The dogs in jubilation
scoured the pile
for familiar objects:
sheet, drawer, handle, doll—
shards of tiny familiar
now exploded
into atoms of scent.

They had no grief
for the larger orders
of entrance, hall, yard.
They had no sorrow
for the geometry.

That was all mine.

GRAVE

"The difference
between house
and home
seems to have been
the moment
we began to bury
our ancestors
near us,"
said the archaeologist,
with an elegance
given only
to those
who touch bones
on a daily basis

Which moment
I asked
as the lights came up

Was it the hour
when the boys
broke the stone
of that grave
in the neighbors' field
and we ran
to put flowers
on the broken slab
for weeks after

Was it the day
we made up
an ancestor
who lay
under the lily patch,
unrelated to us
except in our stories

Was it the month
the dog dragged
a perfect skeleton
of a squirrel
from the cellar
holding it gently
as if afraid
to undo the patterns

Or was it the year
we finally began
singing back
to the voice
behind the door—
the one sending music
long before
we were born

ABOUT THE AUTHOR

LAURIE L. PATTON is the author or editor of ten books in the history and culture of Indian religions, mythology, and theory in the study of religion, and sixty articles in these and related fields. Patton translated the Sanskrit classic, *The Bhagavad Gita*, for Penguin classics series in 2008, and is currently at work on a translation of the Hindu epic, *The Mahabharata*. Her first book of poems, *Fire's Goal: Poems from a Hindu Year*, was published in 2003 with White Cloud Press. Her second, *Angel's Task: Poems in Biblical Time* followed in 2011 from Station Hill Press. She currently serves as President and Professor of Religion at Middlebury.

CPSIA information can be obtained
at www.ICGtesting.com
Printed in the USA
LVOW03s0905190418
574051LV00002B/14/P